Mom, I'm Allright.

Mom, I'm Allright.
CONFESSIONS OF A FORMER
Stripper

MONICA MENDEZ

Mendez, Monica
Mom, I'm Allright. Confessions of a Former Stripper
Copyright © 2009

Salacious Press
A division of BurmanBooks

Printed in Canada

About the Author

Monica Mendez lives in Los Angeles and is now an aspiring photographer.

Day of Judgement

It's amazing how quick people are to judge in a town like Hollywood, particularly those who have no right or place to do so. Yeah yeah, I know, what do I expect, I dance naked for a living.

Sometimes, it turns out, those who judge just happen to work in what I like to call "The Sex Business". Models, actors, actresses, and all your typical "tinsel town extras", who love to come into the club just like any other hot-blooded man or woman. These people sell themselves on a daily basis—on a different stage, and maybe naked only part of the time, but they no doubt sell themselves.

I remember back when I was still doing the whole "actress" thing, I went on many auditions. One in particular will stick with me forever. I was sitting there in the dressing room—I mean, "casting room"—wow, that's a Freudian slip if I've ever heard one—and I started to glance around the room, sizing up the competition, when I noticed a theme throughout the entire line-up. I was the most over-dressed, covered up girl in the room. Every boob job in there came with a matching mini-skirt and complimentary "Tammy Faye" cosmetics kit. And then there was me—jeans with holes, a tank top, and a sinking feeling that I am out of my element. Out of the corner of my eye I noticed a face that I definitely knew, but couldn't remember from where.

Then it hit me—she was at the club not more than a week ago. It was a Friday night and she had clearly been club hopping for hours. At this point, she was a little bit tipsy and extremely obnoxious and annoying. She was a typical female customer—there to please at least one of the 3 guys she came with—the type that will sit stage, not tip, and be sure to annunciate her negative comments on each girl loud enough for all of her friends to hear.

But on this night it backfired. All the attention was on us—the ones she was trying to trash. She had to think fast. Stumbling out of her chair and up to the DJ booth, she decided that she wanted to audition—right there and then. The DJ then proceeded to explain to her that she needed the proper shoes and attire to do it. Sabrina, one of the girls I worked with, donated her highest pair of heels, realizing her chance to finally get even with her and her mouth.

"I'll lend you my stuff sweetie," she said, with a devilish grin—Sabrina was quite the little spitfire. I thought to myself "This is really fucked up," but after hearing her sit at stage all night saying things like "Don't tip her, she's got a hideous boob job" or "Look at her rolls, ugh", it was payback time!

Each of us took it upon ourselves to decorate this girl like a stripper Christmas tree. Fishnet this, leather that—you get the picture and then—it was SHOWTIME! All the girls gathered around the stage to watch their production.

I heard the DJ start to play No Doubt's "I'm Just a Girl"—her pick—Jesus, *she* was just a girl! She made it through, falling only once, but she was so nervous throughout the performance because she'd forgotten to shave.

I find it funny how people judge, but in just a few moments can find themselves on the other side. That night, she made about $40 in just a few minutes and was ecstatic. She had succeeded and managed to impress her friends at the same time.

When I saw her at the audition, she was very serious and focused on her lines. I wasn't about to approach her. This time I was on her turf, in front of her pack—all these girls knew her—just like we were in the dressing room at the club.

Now, I was out of place and felt like I did not belong. So just like her, I left the audition and never came back.

TOY LADIES

Lots of people associate drugs with adult entertainment, and I'd be hard pressed to get you to believe otherwise. So I'm not going to sugarcoat the fact that you have to put yourself in that "bubble" every night—your own little customized force field to help you get through the whole experience.

It's not easy to get up there night after night and sell yourself—and do it with no clothes on to boot. So yeah, sometimes I need a drink, or 3, or something to smoke. Some girls need a little—or a lot—more.

That's where the Toy Ladies come into play—or should I say come in to play. The Toy Ladies were two young ladies who made their living off the nightlife. They were club kids.

Although they rarely made it all the way to the stage, they usually managed to walk away with more money than the rest of us. Girls will definitely pay top dollar when they need a "bubble", especially when they're about to start their shift and are all out at home.

The Toy Ladies were responsible for my first experimentation with drugs. They set up shop in the dressing room with a Kraft services spread, only there wasn't anything to eat—sort of. They would ask each girl "What do you need tonight?" and go down the line.

They were here to make money off us, not the guys who sit out front. These girls stood out, their clothes all bright and flashy—just looking at them was like an acid trip—and elaborate handmade costumes. They were club-ready 24/7 and always made up like they were headed to a photo shoot.

Those nights would come, when you'd say: "No, I'm good, not tonight" and then a few hours later, ask: "What do you have again?" Needless to say, they rarely had a bad night.

These girls made our nights just a little more enjoyable. Not only were their sales skills up to par, but these girls were performers at their finest. Watching them dance on stage was pure pleasure. It was fun. They loved to perform. Whether it was in a gentlemen's club on the east side of town, or a trendy Hollywood club on the Westside, they put one hundred percent into everything that they did, from their costumes, to their late-night partying.

I remember that they always seemed to be going a hundred miles a minute. In a way, I kind of envied them. These girls could care less what people thought of them, which seems to be a common trend with adult entertainers. In this business you just have to learn not to care what people think, because in the end that's what will save you, and the Toy Ladies were no exception. They have survived everything, the drugs, the partying, the strip club lifestyle, and the harsh discrimination that accompanies it.

Not long ago, I ran into one of them on the street. She was almost unrecognizable. She looked different without her club gear on and all grown up. There, in the sidewalk under the harsh California sun, with coffee in hand, a far cry from a dark seedy strip club in the middle of the night with a sugary jack and coke, she began to tell me of her past and present.

After having enough of the club life she decided to start her own legit business. She used her smarts and beauty for something else and became an entrepreneur of a different kind. This toy lady traded in her pink hair, handmade clothes, and over the top club makeup for designer duds and fashionable haircuts, suitable for any powerful woman you would find working on Wall Street.

All the money she had made in the past was put to her future.

And the remaining Toy Lady? She was living the life of a happy housewife, out of Los Angeles. She had traded in the club lifestyle for diapers and a suburban family car. As I walked away from my one-time bubble builder, I could not help but get a little sad. It was like leaving a fun vacation. You're happy to go home, but you're sure going to miss that period of time when you didn't have to worry about bills, cleaning the house, or getting up early for work.

But, sooner or later you have to go home—or in our case, you have to grow up.

DIZZY IZZY

My friend Izzy was the girl next door, literally. After Christy died I just had to get out of Hollywood. It represented a dark time in my life. Since I wasn't dancing at the club or working at the Rainbow, I thought it was a perfect time to live near the beach.

I haven't left since.

The only problem is that it is a lot more costly to live at such a beautiful location. I knew I would have to pick up some nights at the club and get a second restaurant job, on top of going back to school for some classes.

I wanted to find a cheap place with no roommates. That's where Izzy enters the story. I used to work with her years ago at "Century Lounge", the very first club I danced at. She was from Canada and had a very strong French Canadian accent, with a heart to match. Crazy as she is, she'd give you the shirt off her back if she liked you, unless of course it was a KISS shirt. Then, you can forget it. She was and is to this day the #1 KISS fan of all time, along with every other metal band on the list. She took me to my first Ozzy concert and we sat in the front row. What an experience. I've seen many more metal bands since then, but that one will live in my memory forever.

It was right after Christy had died and Papillion had gone back home. I needed an escape, and my good friend Izzy was a perfect fit. She also happened to refer me to her landlord when the apartment next door opened up.

It was almost perfect—close to the beach, dirt cheap, and I could have a pet. My boy Lobo has to have a place to lay his head too. Like it or not, I was embarking on a new and exciting adventure. And, like it or not, I was going to have a roommate, sort of. I could just step out the front door and knock on hers. I remember one night after work—about 3AM—Izzy was crankin' music and had some chicken on the BBQ, like it was the fourth of July or something.

"Hey babe, you hungry?" she asked. After a quick "What the fuck is she doing at 3AM making all this noise and grilling?" to myself I replied, "Hell yeah, I'm starving!"

She was great—never a dull moment with her around. I remember one time I had a friend coming over for dinner. He walked up to our building and happened to see Izzy out front gardening.

"Oh I love gardening, what are you planting?" he asked. "Oh babe" she replied, "these are fake plants from the 99 cent store. I don't have time to deal with the real thing."

Now I don't know which is crazier, the fact that she was gardening in the middle of the night or that she was planting plastic plants in the flowerbeds. After I moved from that building I really missed little stuff like that. She always gave you something to take with you—a strange little event that you'd never ever forget.

Izzy was and is a true friend and I'm glad she was

there during that period in my life. She made sure that if I did get upset, it would not last more than a minute. I recommend everybody having an Izzy in his or her life. I lived next to Izzy in that apartment for about two years, and in that time I rediscovered myself. I discovered the photographer in me, the artist in me, and how much passion I had for it.

I fell in love with a boy and got engaged for about six months. And when he broke my heart, Izzy was there once again to put a smile on my face.

THE BUNNY MAN

It was an early day shift. There wasn't a soul in sight and barely enough light to keep the bartender awake. I looked up and in came a thin African American man about 6 feet tall with his hands precariously cradling something.

I wasn't quite sure what to make of it, so I just kept an eye on him for a while, making sure he was, you know, all there. Well, it turns out he wasn't. Or maybe he was—that depends on how you look at it.

He walked over to a table near the back, looking sultry and sexy, moving cat-like. I had to find out what was going on with this guy, and what the hell was he hiding under his arm. At that moment, Lucky, a sexy redhead happened to walk up and sit down beside me. She looked at me, noticing my gaze in his direction, and smiled.

"So, have you two met?" she asked.

I looked at her.

"Who? Him?"

"That's the Bunny Man," she told me.

"The Bunny Man?" I asked, frowning, "What the fuck are you talking about?"

"That's the guy with the rabbit," she said.

At that point I didn't know what to think. Did this guy walk in here with a fucking live bunny rabbit? He brings his pet with him to get lap dances? What a fucking wack-job! She continued to tell me that it would be far more reasonable if that were the case. You see, it turns out that this guy is, well, I guess you could say that his walk says a lot about him. You don't meet too many homosexual males in a gentlemen's club, and if you do, you had better be prepared. He has a friend, his stuffed bunny that he brings with him to watch the girls strip. Why? Well, sometimes people just can't get a grip on their sexuality, and other times they just can't get a grip…period! This bunny looked like it had been through more shit than all of us girls put together. The eyes had been re-attached, and very poorly by the way. The damn thing looked cross-eyed and there was stuffing popping out everywhere. It looked like he ran it over with a tractor before he came in. It turns out the bunny represents Leroy's heterosexual side because he, himself, is gay. Not just gay, but on fire like the San Fernando Valley mid-summer gay. The girls do dances for the bunny and he talks to it while they do, asking if the bunny "likes that" and "wants some more". The entire time Lucky is telling me this, she seems completely unaffected by him, like this is just another day at the office and people come in all the time with stuffed animals that want to get lap dances. She urges me to go over and meet him saying "He spends money. He's a good customer". She says that I shouldn't be afraid of him. I politely respond with "That's a little too weird for me, thanks" and start to look around for a dance. Hours pass. It's a so-so night and I end up walking with some bills paid and a bite to eat. Just as I'm walking out, Lucky says "Hey Mo, wanna grab a bite? It's on me." With a so-so night behind me, and hunger pains in my stomach I cant resist a free meal. "Sure, why not?" As I walk over to where the happy red head is standing, She opens her bag to show me over $500 she made that night. In disbelief, cigarette dangling from my mouth I gazed down at her crisp dollar bills. " So, Chinese or Mexican?" she asks. All I could say was, damn, I should have talked to that rabbit.

THE STEREOTYPE

Tonight started off like any other night. I wake up from my siesta at about 5PM. You see, due to the lifestyle, I'm up 'til at least, I'd say 4AM. I come home from work, shower, eat, check my email and maybe have a glass of wine accompanied by some lovely smoke…All this just to unwind and be able to relax and disconnect. But, I don't sleep in all day. I like to get up at around 10AM, and that is very early considering my work schedule. I try my best to be a part of the real world for a brief moment.

Then I take a nap for an hour or two, maybe three, in order to be refreshed for the upcoming night. I live almost like a vampire, except we suck money out of our victims rather than blood. But, tonight was different than most. I just didn't feel like going in. Today I found that I had just become a little more overwhelmed with my bills, and subsequently lost it. I was truly a wreck. I started to have one of those "stripper" moments. One where I become encased in this shell of self-doubt and regret, only to be followed by the ever-haunting question—"Now what the fuck am I going to do?" Everyone has those moments where you question everything you have done, will do, and are thinking about doing someday. You get depressed and down on yourself, and sometimes it evolves from down on yourself to I hate myself. Everyone has different reasons why they sit there and tell themselves they are a failure and why they can't look in the mirror today. We hate that our moms don't know what we do and are afraid that if they did, they wouldn't accept us. We hate that people who matter to us far less than our moms, people in the clubs, on the street, complete strangers, think we are terrible people because of what we do. I hate myself when I tell someone what I do. I try to be honest and I feel no shame or guilt at the time, but when they look at me you can see it. It's like the skin is slowly slipping from my body. They know absolutely nothing about who I really am as a person. I hate when I turn on the radio and some disc jockey is telling women to flash their breasts in traffic to a bunch of lonely losers who can't get a date to save their life (we won't name any names, but he doesn't *lyke us*), the whole time telling them not to date strippers because we're 2nd class, hell 3rd class citizens. I hate when I think that I've finally found Mr. Right, only to find out later that he can't deal with what I do. That's fine, but 2 days later to find him in some other strip joint acting like an idiot—what the fuck……get over yourself Poindexter! The worst one of all—I hate when some dumb bitch decides to take her job of "entertaining" too far and let some guy grab her tits for $20, or do a lot more nowadays. Great, now we're all looked at as prostitutes because she's too ugly to earn the money on her looks alone. I'm a dancer not a fucking hooker you stupid whore! And lastly, for now, I hate it when a group of assholes comes in to the club with a mission—Treat every girl like complete shit and maybe we'll get some. Wake up moron. Just because you have to get up in the morning and hear your nagging wife whining about how you can't please her and you can't do this or that, then sit in rush-hour traffic to get to a job you absolutely can't stand, and then come in to the club only to spend all that hard earned money on little 'ol me while I lie to your face about how good looking you are, is no reason to get feisty. Now, who's the idiot in this scenario Einstein? We all go through hard times in our life, whether we are doctors, actors, lawyers, or strippers. Shit happens and you have to carry your own freaking scooper pal. I chose this job, and chose yours. Find something that makes the downtime worth it. For me it's my camera. I like to pick it up and capture emotions on film, in the dressing room, around town, wherever. It feels good to take a picture and see in someone's eyes that they feel the same as me. They go through the same stuff, day in day out. In the end I know that I am not just a stripper, I am just another struggling artist trying to pay the bills.

THE ACID TRIP

OK. So I can't say that I'm a novice when it comes to drugs. The first time I smoked pot I was in high school. I think I was 15 at the time, and I loved it! Hell, I went to high school in Canada. Everyone loved it! High school in Canada was great for me. I love that my high school days were spent in Canada. To this day I believe that going to high school in Canada as opposed to somewhere in L.A. It molded me into what I am today. A retired stripper trying to make it as an artist while surviving on low-cost, budget meals and thrift stores to supply the clothes on her back—and loving every minute of it. Sure, everybody loves money, and most folks would do just about anything to get it. Hell, I took my clothes off for it. But it was never for some expensive car or jewelry, or some purse that everyone else says is cool. It was just to survive comfortably, which could lead me down the path to happiness. I never stripped for a drug habit either. I mean, sure, I got my share of pot from the "Toy Ladies", but at the time, I was only familiar with weed, magic mushrooms, LSD, and alcohol. At 21 years old, this was my history in the world of the experimental. Most of this I had done in high school and shortly thereafter. I did try coke once on my 21st birthday and I hated it! I never touched the stuff again. It wasn't really around much in our high school. My younger brother, on the other hand, lived in and attended high school in L.A. and experienced a lot more than me. My reaction when I came upon friends with heroin or speed addictions was a bit different than your average inner city kid's probably was. I witnessed beautiful lives completely destroyed right in front of me. LSD. This one leaves some stories behind. One night I came into work and everyone was bored, including the management and door guys. I noticed that some of the girls were passing around some acid. "Black Pyramids" they were called. Once it had made it around to me, I decided to partake since I had such a fond memory of this drug from Canada. I placed it on my tongue and waited while I watched the other girls perform on stage. As time passed the girls became creeping, crawling animals on that stage, stretching their bodies out like cats. It was one of the best trips I had ever had. On my way to pick my music for my next set I noticed a regular sitting at one of the tables, so I decided to go over and say hi. As I got closer I noticed he had a bird sitting beside him, a white dove. I thought it was weird, but oh well. I went to shake his hand and the bird jumped off the table toward me! I jumped back, startled! "Are you OK?" he asked. When I calmed myself down enough to ask him "What the hell is your bird doing in here?" I noticed that it wasn't a bird at all. It was a used napkin that appeared to fly off the table at me. I realized that the acid had taken control of my senses and quickly dismissed myself from the table. I ran off without a goodbye and didn't even look back to see the look on his face. I'm sure he was just convinced that all strippers were just crazy. But now I had to deal with the fact that I was up next. So on comes "I am the Walrus" and I find myself on stage. It was time to express myself, my favorite part of dancing, and I was trippin', hard!

THE SAN FRANCISCO TREAT

I was one year into dancing when I was first approached by a photographer. OK, a model who introduced me to a photographer. She was a feature dancer who was using her Penthouse centerfold credits to headline some of the biggest men's clubs in Hollywood. This is usually how burnt out porn stars and centerfold models continue to make money after the glory days are over. The magazines and photographers stop calling because, well, because there's nothing left to see. They're used up, washed out, and thrown to the wolves. Cue the sleazy "I'm an agent who books feature dancers all over the country" dirtbag. These are the guys who think they can make any girl the next Jenna. They come in, crammed into some undersized Hawaiian shirt with a Jimmy Buffet logo, and start spouting off how much cash you can make as a feature dancer if they handle your "career". What they don't tell you is that it's all shit! It's a lonely life, even lonelier than being a house dancer, if you can imagine that. When I was approached, I had already shot for some Playboy layouts and for some of their newsstand editions. This dancer told me about a female photographer by the name of Suze Randall, one of the best female photographers in the adult industry. I wasn't making enough money with the Playboy stuff and they had turned me down as a Playmate. And as far as acting went, I tried it and got bored fairly quickly. Going to audition after audition, having to listen to a bunch of thespians talk about all the jobs they're not getting and how they're living on Cup o' Noodles week after week. It's like listening to a broken fucking record! So, I decided to meet the photographer of choice in the adult world. Now, I went into the nude modeling business with an open mind, but with limitations as well. I only wanted to pose nude alone, or with another girl, if it was done tastefully (if you consider 2 girls fondling each other on a haystack tasteful). Nevertheless, I was soon, as Suze put it, being thrown into the deep end. Days later I found myself on the set, being photographed nude for the world to see, and many other shoots were to follow. Before I knew what was happening, I was washed up. I had posed for so many magazines that no photographers would shoot me unless I went into the more explicit, edgy stuff, and that was just not for me. It was just a matter of time before the fat, Hawaiian shirt guy found me. And he did, right on time. My first feature gig went great. I toured the U.S. OK, I toured Michigan, San Francisco, Vegas, and L.A. Not quite the U.S. but the parts where I could make some scratch. San Francisco, I had been there before, to the same club. The money and clientele were not as good as Michigan and some others, but I loved the city. It is a beautiful place to see, and they are very liberal there, including the clubs I danced in. After my shows I would generally leave, as opposed to sticking around and selling posters or pics or whatever. Next door there was this little dive bar owned by 2 Scottish lesbians, which is where I spent my breaks in between sets, playing pool and drinking bourbon with the locals. This was my mandatory stop both before and after every show, to "recharge" my bubble, unwind, and let go of all the negativity inside. Billiards and bourbon equals relaxation, and maybe some pot too.

Aahhh, good 'ol Mary Jane. On the night of my last show it was going to be a bit different. It was Friday, so instead of 15 or 18 guys, there would be 100+, all fans of mine and all there to see a show. 100 people may not sound like many, but it is for a strip club. Let's face it, I have a fan base, not a "fame" base like some girl with 34FFF's who starred in "Creampie Sluts Vol. 37" or something like that. I'm a centerfold model so I have a small fan base, but when Friday night rolls around, they expect to be entertained. As I walked into the mandatory pre-show venue to recharge, I recognized an old friend that I had met last time I was in town. He was older who had hitchhiked over to the U.S. in the sixties as a teenager and never left the bar, except probably for Woodstock. He was still wearing the same tye-dye t-shirt he came to San Fran in. He had great smoke and could play a mean game of eight ball though. And believe me, I could use both. I asked if he had some on him and he replied with "Man, I got something even better, man" in his best Tommy Chong voice. With a glossy twinkle in his eye and day old nicotine on his breath he leaned over and handed me what appeared to be a tiny little Visine bottle. Well, that's exactly what it was; only there was nothing for your eyes in it. It was pure liquid THC. I took the bottle to the ladies room to partake……one, two, three, and a fourth drop on the tongue for good luck. Then I made my way back to the pool table and my lonely beer. As I continued to play, I noticed that every stroke of the pool cue was accompanied by a short wave of dizziness and warmth throughout my entire body. The music on the juke box was starting to fade off into the distance like a car passing by, and everyone was staring at me, or so it seemed. In seconds I went from "This is great" to "Get me the hell out of here!", but I had to go on for my final show. I couldn't go home or leave. As I sat in my dressing room, paranoia settled in. Why am I here? The nice stoner high that had so many times saved me from the darkness of the stage had now sucked me into a pit of overwhelming fear. Holy shit I was high!!—Too high to pick a costume, and too high to pick my music, which was one of the most enjoyable parts of the show preparation. I was even too high to set my stage up, to light the candles and set the props. I didn't pay some roadie to come handle that shit for me. I did it myself. I tried to get myself together and realized that most of my costumes were fairly elaborate, all except one. The "American girl" costume. Yeah, that's right, the ultimate stripper "must have" get up. Great for Middle America if you're dancing to Springsteen or something you might hear blaring out of the window of an F150 on an old dirt road, but not for Frisco. But oh well, I was too stoned to consider that, I was just happy that I could figure out what was the front and what was the back. I just wanted to make it through this last show and get the hell out of there. The closer show time got, the higher I became. I heard the DJ running through my list of credits on the sound system before announcing me to the stage. Beads of sweat were devastating my poorly done make-up job, I took a drag off of my cigarette hoping it would calm me down only to find that it intensified my cotton mouth ten fold. As I made my way past the crowd with the lights hitting me, I could not help but laugh. Oh shit! A laughing fit right as my set is starting. The stage was no longer my safe place. It was where I was going to hang myself in front of a bunch of angry villagers. They would cheer as I fell to my death and the music would play in the streets. By the time I got to the stage I could hear nothing but the beating of my heart, and I froze. On stage and paralyzed, every performer's worst nightmare come true. The little Visine bottle had defeated me. I'm having a stroke, I'm going to faint, what do I do? I knelt down on stage and could not look up at the audience. They must be in shock, I know I am! I'm sweating through my red, white and blue spandex costume like a WWF wrestler and cannot move. All I could think of was getting off that stage. My subtle "stand up and walk off" became "run like there's no tomorrow". As I ran toward the dressing room I saw the looks on the crowd's faces. The DJ was scrambling to get a house girl on stage and I was fumbling with the lock to my dressing room. Finally I made it inside and sat down. I looked in the mirror and wondered what went wrong, chain smoking and plotting my escape. The walls were really thin and I could hear the whispers just outside, and then a knock. "Monica, are you OK?" the manager asked. At this point I had such bad cotton mouth, I could hardly answer. Just then my prayers were answered. The security guy came in and told me that the manager had asked him to walk me back to my hotel. The manager was so pissed he wouldn't even talk to me, but the security guy was cool. After walking me back and reassuring me that I was not going to die, he left so I could sleep it off. The next morning, before leaving town, I stopped by the club to pick up my check. As I left I noticed out of the corner of my eye that the girl from "Creampie Sluts Vol. 37" was walking in. Enjoy the show, I'm out of here.

ARE YOU A NORMAL GIRL OR DO YOU WORK HERE?

It was about a year after retiring from dancing when an old friend called me up and asked to meet for a drink. I said yes and we decided to go to a local bikini bar for some drinks and pool. We hadn't seen each other in quite some time and I was really looking forward to catching up. You might be asking "Why would 2 girls who used to dance for a living meet up for drinks at a strip club?" Well, cheap drinks for one, a good variety of music, cheap billiard tables, and we actually enjoy watching girls dance, if they are good at it. And last but not least, we figure if there are half naked girls dancing on stage we won't be bothered as much. That's how it usually goes anyway, until that 1 drunk bastard finally realizes that MOST of these girls are dancers, not hookers, and that he's not going to flash some ones and end up scoring a trophy wife….Which leaves him with the "I'll just talk to the girls who are here to enjoy themselves and hang out" approach. Brilliant! When you see 2 women in a strip club as customers, one would assume that they are probably lesbians and don't want to be bothered by anyone but the girls on stage and the cocktail waitress. But the guys that are there, because there is no other hope for them, I mean, they can't go to a regular bar and expect a women to talk to them there. So they retreat to a strip club where for the right amount of money any girl will talk to them. And when they realize that they are not going to find a date, or the bank accounts run dry, which ever comes first, they turn to the girls hanging out.

This particular night was no exception. It was nearing the end of the evening and Morgan (my friend) thought we had survived the evening without any interruptions. Just then my nose got a whiff of the over whelming scent of cheap cologne. By the time I turned my head to see what was attached to the distinct smell I felt the touch of a cold clammy hand on my bare shoulder. "So are you girls normal, or do you work here?" Now you can imagine what went through my head when he asked this question. In such shock that some one would even ask such a question we both just sat there jaws wide open in disgust. I guess the word "normal" can be taken many ways but this guy thought he had a chance, and that's really, really abnormal!

WHEN YOUR BUBBLE BURSTS

I always talk about this bubble that most dancers, myself included, create in order to cope with the job. For some that bubble is built with pure PMA, and for some it is built with pure inebriation. Eventually that bubble is going to pop though, it happens to the best of us. In the beginning, I used to go into work and enjoy it. Having some smoke or a couple cocktails was just an added bonus. Especially working at the world famous Body Shop on the Sunset Strip in Hollywood. Just like the Crüe sang about in the song "Girls, Girls, Girls", it was the place to be on any Friday night in L.A., but when you're 19, 20, 21 years old in Tinseltown, you don't slow down to think about the outcome of your choices, you just go for it. Someone offers you a shot, you take it. You have to become sexy, seductive, and entertaining all at once, and on top of it, you are naked, if not fully, than damn near. That's when that shot sounds so good, and the second, and the third, you get the picture. Before you know it, it becomes part of your routine, and for some it becomes an addiction. Near the end of my dancing "career" it was rough. I found myself trying to find clubs that were really low-key, or where no one even knew me or had ever seen me. It wasn't the same anymore. I didn't have Christy or Pap around to make it all make sense somehow. I found myself alone, trying to start my life over. I was going to college during the day studying photography and film, waiting tables for catering gigs occasionally, and dancing at night in between for extra cash. I had found this tiny club near the airport that fit the profile just right, so I decided to work there once, maybe twice a week depending on school and other projects. This time things would be different. I wasn't just a dancer. I was a student, a photographer, a waitress, and dancing would just be my little something extra—my little secret. I didn't have to depend on it night after night to pay my bills. I wouldn't have to go to bed with sore knees, an aching back, and the soles of my feet on fire, only to have to psych myself out to make it back the next night. The first night in the new club was going great until, in walked a familiar face. It was a dancer that I had worked with way back in the beginning of this episode of my life. She was a little older than me, probably in her mid to late 30's. She was a really tall blonde with some of the most perfect implants you've ever seen. In fact, everything she owned was perfect. Her car was a brand new Lexus, worth more than everything I owned 3 times over. And then her condo, all she talked about was how perfectly decorated it was. Oh, and let's not forget about the clothes, the jewelry, and those purses—Those ugly ass purses. Ladies, let me get off the subject for just a moment here to vent. Impulse buys where you spend hundreds, maybe even thousands of dollars on something so small and insignificant amazes me. I always get a kick out of watching some, not all, but some of these girls in the dressing room gush over these little hand bags that look like they came from the "Maude Adams" designer collection. They ran out and bought it because of the name on the little gold buckle that no one can see or differentiate from the fake ones sold down at the beach. Some of these girls would take an entire week's pay and blow it on a purse like that. It's hysterical that someone would spend so much on something that holds money. Is there anything left to put in it now? Anyways, back to this dancer. She was definitely one of these girls. She loved to make lots of money almost as much as she loved to spend it. I don't know, maybe it made her feel better about herself. Maybe she was trying to spend away her guilt she felt for how she earned the money in the first place. Well, regardless of the reason why, I always felt this underlying sadness when I saw her. Underneath all the expensive clothes and jewelry was a very lonely person. And now, seeing her after all this time, loneliness was all you could see. She still had all that fancy shit she threw her money at, but in her eyes was a deep void that anyone could plainly see. I just wanted to go over and hug her and tell her it doesn't have to be this way. Life is too short to live that way. Instead of toys, good 'ol JD had taken their place. Something that, in the past, had been used to take the edge off had become her addiction, and her bubble that once protected her had popped. She was no longer safe and sheltered from the negativity. It was eating her alive like a pack of wolves on a carcass. As the night went on I noticed she was getting more and more intoxicated, and she had made a bed from all her overpriced costumes and outfits. She had made a "clear" decision that it was time to pass out, and she should definitely use a few thousand dollars worth of ridiculous costumes to create a makeshift bed. Everyone just kind of walked by ignoring her, like it was an everyday occurrence, and from the looks of it, it was her routine thing. That was it, her life was this. It didn't appear that she had a relationship or someone to go home to. There had been some men in her life, but they never intended to stick around. I remember her telling me a long time ago about a certain fellow she had met at the club, but we all know how that turns out. After about a half hour she woke up and got her second wind. I was in the restroom washing my hands when she walked in. "Hey, how's your night going?" she asked. "Pretty good" I replied. In the middle of our dialogue she whipped out a vial of coke and began to try to wake herself up. "Want a bump?" she asked. "No thanks" I said. As I mentioned, that was just never my thing, ever. Under the fluorescent light I could see the line where her makeup started and stopped. "You know, this is not what I wanted. I always wanted to be a veterinarian. I love animals!" she said, out of nowhere. She began telling me her life story. "When I was 5 my mom bought me a puppy. It was the greatest day of my life. I named her Ginger and walked and brushed her everyday. She loved me..." as she went on her eyes began to tear up, and she just stared at herself in the mirror. "One day I came home and she was gone. My dad told me she ran away but I knew that was bullshit. She would have never done that. She loved me, you know?" I didn't know where this story was headed or why she was telling me this, but I felt her pain for sure. She never forgave her father for that, among many other things. After a brief pause she looked at me and asked if I had a dog. I replied "yes". "Cool" she said. "I'll see you out there" and she walked out. I guess life is never perfect.

GUIDELINES

Everyday I sit with my cup of coffee or glass of red wine depending on my mood, on my balcony preparing to write or watch passing traffic, and everyday I notice the same little old man on the same daily routine. He walks every morning to the liquor store for a pack of smokes and then passes by again on his way back to his place. He looks to be in his late 70's, maybe even mid 80's, and is always dressed to perfection, wearing most likely the same suit he wore back in his glory years. His face is aged and bears tracks, like a road map of his life, but you can tell that in his younger years he was very handsome. He is always nicely dressed just to go to the corner store. One time I saw him wearing a turquoise suit with matching shoes, and freshly dyed black hair under his stylish little cigar hat. I wondered what he was like at my age. I imagine him to be this strapping ladies man, running amuck through the Hollywood nightlife, back when it was a glamorous place to be and be seen—When it was dripping with starlets and wealth. What goes through his head now when he walks down the boulevard, only to find souvenir shops and strip joints, tattoo parlors and dive bars? It's no secret that Hollywood has changed, along with the lifestyles of the younger folks who live there. Change is expected in life, but one thing will never change. Everyone gets old, and everyone rethinks their past, wondering what they should have done and what they should not have done. As I watched the old man fade away down the street, I asked myself, is that going to be me? Will I be the old lady, still wearing my youth on my back, with nothing but a daily trip to the corner store to look forward to? Will I grow old alone? If I do, will it be because of the choices I have made in my life? Will any man ever take me serious enough to marry me? Will I ever take myself serious enough? When I meet young girls coming into this industry for the first time, I want nothing more than to sit them down and tell them the truth. Don't spend all your money on cars and clothes, plan for your future, and be smart early so you can enjoy it later and sooner. But, then again, who am I to lecture right? I'm a 32 year old photographer/writer starting from scratch, and have just now started to recognize what it means to truly be happy. Yes, your past does reflect onto your future, but it doesn't have to scar it. If you are thinking about jumping into the adult industry or becoming an exotic dancer, here are a few guidelines to make the landing a bit softer.

#1—**Have a plan.** Know that dancing or posing nude doesn't last forever, and that you do need something to fall back on or work towards. Whether it is the college degree that dancing paid for, or creating a business around your life experiences, use the business, don't let the business use you. A great friend told me that once and I listened, and I have lived by it ever since.

#2—**Find someone you trust to handle your money for you.** It doesn't matter if it is an accountant, a friend, or a family member; just find someone to help you manage your money. This is something that I truly wish I had done from the beginning. No matter what anyone says, this is a business, and you need to treat it like one. The girls who did it the right way have retired early, and gotten respect for it, even from those who disagree with the lifestyle.

#3—Don't push it. Don't overwork yourself. In the beginning you are drawn to the money and you force yourself to work all the time. You forget about the real world going on outside the club, and can lose sight of what you were really meant to discover. Your passion will go unnoticed because you are engulfed in chasing the dollar night after night.

THE 3 MUSKETEERS

When you are young, barely 21, and living in Hollywood you seem to have an easier time making friends. The kind of friends that you "experience" things with or "run amuck" with. They're your true "partners in crime". For me that was Papillion and Christy. There were others I hung around with, but these two I had a real connection with from the moment we met. Now in my thirties, I look back and wonder if I will ever have friends like that again. Like a bad break-up, when it's all said and done and they're all gone, you find yourself afraid to bond like that again, afraid to lose that again. Nothing will ever come close, so why bother. When you build a friendship with another dancer it's more than just sharing each other's clothes and going out on Friday nights sipping cosmos and talking about boys. It's about sharing anger, pain, and tears when the sadness is so bad that all you can do is cry your eyes out. When you work as an exotic dancer, your idea of "partying" is a bit different than most. We preferred staying home most nights. We lived at a little place we liked to call "The Whiskey House"—the name says it all. It was right above Franklin, which is right above Hollywood, which is right above Sunset…you get the picture. And if you don't, well then let me elaborate. We lived smack dab in the middle of the shit! We were pretty much walking distance from all the bars, clubs, restaurants, liquor stores, where the runway junkies hovered the store like a flock of seagulls waitin' for a fat man to drop a Dorito. It was right near the tourist laden streets of Hollywood Boulevard, where people from all over the world walked up and down, day and night, hoping for a glimpse of a celebrity amongst the head shops and freaks looking for a fix. The Whiskey House was a retreat…our escape from, well everything. The party somehow always made its way to us. No waiting in line, no getting dressed up. Just great food, wine, friends, and of course, whiskey. Sometimes our friends who played music would come over and jam. Some could play, and some, well they tried. Regardless, we were a family. Christy's family, at the time, wasn't really on speaking terms and Pap's family lived too far away. All I had was my mom, but she lived hours away. We all knew that our families wouldn't approve of the way we chose to pay our bills, so we had our own little family to support each other.

I first met Christy at the Century Lounge. She was a cocktail waitress/dancer, and I was just getting my feet in the door, and living in Venice Beach at the time. We were from 2 completely different worlds. She played on the streets of L.A. and I played in the sand and surf of

Venice. She was the most beautiful girl I had ever seen. She was confident, adventurous, and loving…. a follower not a leader. I envied her freedom immediately, but like myself, there was a part of her that was hurting. She did a very good job of hiding it, but there were days when the sadness was much to too strong to hide. Then there was Papillion, the French butterfly; she was tall and thin with thick long brown hair and a sexy French accent to match. When I first met Pappy, as I like to call her, she was going through a breakup with her boyfriend and was staying in a very undesirable hotel on Sunset Blvd. One night she needed a ride home from work so another dancer and I drove her home. As I followed her up the stairs while trying not to step on the junkies sitting on the stairs, I wondered how such a nice girl ended up here. Sometimes people come to Hollywood expecting fancy hotels on every block, big houses in Beverly Hills, and the celebrities that live in them lacing the streets. What they don't expect to find are a lot of seedy hotels and the cracked out hookers that live in them.

When I got to her room, I could not believe my eyes, WHAT A SHITHOLE! The carpet looked like it had not been washed or changed since the seventies. The walls had a dirty yellowish tint from years of cigarette smoke. And the bed, lets just say after a quick five-second glance, I could only imagine who and what had been on that polyester floral bedspread. I made my way over to the curtains that matched the bedspread, " Maybe if we open these curtains, we can get some sunlight in". As I swung open the dusty curtains a pigeon flew out and the only light coming in was from the other seedy hotel right next to it. She couldn't stay here; I couldn't let this nice girl from a different country fresh out of a long relationship stay in a place like this. Something was just telling me to help this person out. It would come to be one of the best decisions I ever made. The second would be helping Christy out when she needed a place to live. Before I knew it, the three of us were sharing everything, and when I say everything I mean everything. We shared a small one bedroom in Venice, we shared car rides to and from work, like most girls we shared clothes, and like most girls we shared heartache. I grew up without sisters, now I would finally know what it was like to have them.

I have met a lot of girls since then, but I never got close, like I did with these two. We were a family. The only thing missing was the blood. When I look back and wonder what my life would have been like without them in it, I start to almost panic. Now that they're not here, at times I feel a little incomplete, empty, like something is missing. And I began to feel this way from the minute I received the phone call telling me that Christy was gone....That she had passed away while I was at my grandmother's funeral. One night, that's all it took, and she was gone. Aside from losing two amazing grandparents, this would be a rough loss for me. It was rough for many, but Papillion and I were losing a sister, a musketeer had fallen. After that, it was rough and things were changing. We didn't work at the club anymore. It just had too many bad memories, or should I say good memories, which in return made it hard. Everything reminded us about her, a certain song, and her locker in the dressing room. Before she had died I was living right next to her in the same apartment complex. I remember standing in her apartment when she was gone, trying to take it all in one last time. Getting one last whiff of her China Rain oil that she would dowse herself in every morning. Taking in all the memories one last time, for future reference.

Shortly after, I moved back to Venice, went back to school, got a regular job and tried to begin a new life. Papillion went and tried to stick it out, but eventually after a failed relationship, she decided to go home. Once again, another musketeer had fallen, and I was alone. Sometimes I have this dream at night were I am sitting in a church with Christy and we are laughing and having a good time just like we used to. Then there is silence and she turns to me, smiles, and says "Thank you for coming to my funeral, it was beautiful". Then I wake up. I never get a chance to thank her for coming into my life, and making it beautiful.

ACCEPTING YOUR PATH

When you decide it's time to change your life or crossover from the adult entertainment business, or any other form of nude entertainment, the first thing you have to do is accept your past choices. I don't want to say, "forgive" your past, because unless you hurt or betrayed yourself or someone else along the way, there's nothing to forgive. There are girls that have succeeded in this business, and by succeed I mean that they are happy with themselves and their job. They have accepted the hand they were dealt and have made the best of it. They have come clean with their family and friends about the choices they've made. These are the girls I have always admired. The girls with the "Fuck you, this is me, take it or leave it" attitude. Unfortunately in this society, most people would choose to leave it, but are those really people with the character you look for in a person? I heard that if you are honest, people tend to forgive you, and if you are in denial, people can see right through it. I remember sitting around on so many photo shoots having to listen to model after model run their mouths about their career choices. They were insistent that everyone around them knew that they're "not a porn star" or that they don't do "real porn". It was like they wanted the whole block to hear it just in case someone thought they were.

One time on the set of a well known website shoot I was working with 2 other models. One was from overseas and fairly new in the business, so she decided to turn to one of the more experienced girls for some advice. One of the other models couldn't stop talking about herself and how much money she makes and how she's a celebrity, so the girl from overseas naturally went to her for some information. It was during lunch when the "novice" decided to approach the "celebrity" model for some answers to her questions. It wasn't really what she asked but more how she asked it that set the bragging model through the roof.

"How did you become so successful in the pornography business?" she asked. It was like she had been asked how she made so much money off of skinning puppies. You could see her eyes start to twitch and an inferno of rehearsed vocabulary starting to rush to the tip of her ignorant tongue. "Look, I'm a nude model, not a porn star. I don't do porn!" she said. All I wanted to say to her was to step out of her huge steaming pile of denial, and it may just be time to accept what she does for a living. I am so tired of women, or in this case, little girls, in the adult business carrying on with this high and mighty attitude. Newsflash ladies, just because you haven't had sex with a man on film doesn't mean you're not a porn star. They put themselves on this pedestal like they're freakin' fashion models working for Elle magazine. Let's face it. Although I do believe that adult models and high fashion models are the same, in the sense that they both have a career selling sex, female adult models sell sex primarily to men and fashion models sell sex to both men and women, in a much more tame and censored manner.

I used to get defensive when people would refer to me as a porn star too. Then one day I looked up the definition of pornography, and suddenly it was clear that I was young, naïve, and ignorant. I was ashamed for not being honest with myself. I wasn't ashamed for what I had done and I'm still not. I was just mad because the reason I was not making progress in my life is that I was being a coward. I just wanted to stand up in a crowded restaurant and yell, "Yes, I've done porn. That does not make me a monster!" I have posed in Playboy, and yes I consider that to be pornography of a certain kind as well. Some, not all, but some Playmates are the worst for carrying on this way. I remember when I was waiting tables at the Rainbow on sunset, you use to get a lot of rock stars and Playmates or PORNSTARS, you might call them. One busy Friday night, I noticed a familiar face. It was a model that had been working the Playboy circuit. She was a busty, not natural, blonde. Her hair extensions looked as if they had been placed there back in the eighties along with the orange tan. I remember her from one particular shoot where she sat there at lunch insulting another model for doing Penthouse and other men's magazines. "I can't believe she would do porn like that, doesn't she have any respect for herself!" As she sat at the table stuffing her face with the Kraft service delight, she quickly reassured my belief of the overwhelming ignorance that surrounds this industry.

When I recognized this model at the Rainbow, I noticed that she was in the company of a certain fellow who was known for being accompanied by lots of lovely ladies. And they were not there for his good looks if you know what I mean. From what I heard he paid very well for a good night of company. Now, if this is what a girl chooses to do for a living fine, I am surely not one to judge, but these girls have no right to judge. Just like the old saying goes, "People who live in glass houses should not throw stones."

MOM, I REALLY AM OK

When I started to write this book, one word kept creeping into my thoughts—Honesty. No matter what I was going to be honest. I figured, not everyone has to agree with or enjoy this book; I just have to be real with myself. One thing this job has given me is some thick fucking skin. I want people to know the truth about this gig, good or bad. A lot of the stories you'll read in this book I had never spoken of until now. Not even to the one person that matters to me the most—my mother. This is the one person that when I look her in the face, it kills me to not be able to tell her the truth. So where does she think I work? Well, I also waited tables at the time, and she was aware of the occasional modeling job with Playboy. I know that there are a lot of girls out there who, like me, have been unable to be truthful with their mothers and it eats them up inside. Some have mothers like mine, women that we look up to and, are great people and even greater moms. I remember when I was in high school and living in Canada with my mom after her divorce, we used to drive by the local strip club and stare when we stopped at the red light. The girls were sitting outside smoking in their high heels and my mother would say, "They have no respect for themselves". It's funny but I never saw it that way. I just saw girls who didn't give a shit what people might think of them. Maybe they were just trying to find out who they were. My mother is a very strong and independent lady. I never in my life, even being around so many women, ever met one tougher or braver. She pretty much raised 2 children alone without the help of my father.

My father left when I was about ten, or should I say my mother left him. When you are that young, you remember it in pieces. Kind of like a bad dream. I remember the other woman, that he said was just a good friend. I remember one Thanksgiving he said that mom had to work so we were going to his "FRIEND'S" house for dinner. Only to come home and find my mom passed out on the couch with a dinner going cold and stale just like our family. Before I knew it she had the bags and car packed and headed for home…

Canada. Don't get me wrong, my father is not a bad guy, I do believe that the time he served as a young soldier in Vietnam fucked him up. Two tours to be exact, only to come home and work for the police force, which in LA is not any better. I know what you're thinking, most strippers or adult stars come from broken homes or BAD DADDIES, and you may be right. But I will tell you one thing, I have a good mommy, and she raised me right. Yeah sure, I turned out to be an adult entertainer, but that was my decision.

HE LOVES ME…MAYBE NOT

Yes, trying to find a mate in Hollywood is tough, well, anything long term that is. Everywhere you go there is someone beautiful. In Hollywood, late-night romps are just as tempting as a walk-on role on Desperate Housewives, and just as meaningless. It makes it really hard for men, and women, to settle for just one lover. In my case, throw in the fact that you take off your clothes for a living, and you make the challenge a bit harder. I guess you could say we are not exactly girlfriend material, although I would strongly argue this point.

I remember catching some documentary about "Rock and Roll wives" or something like that, and they interviewed all these different rockers and their ex and current wives, showcasing the trials and tribulations associated with the party life. One by one they explained the temptations of Hollywood, the big 3, as I "like to call 'em: Sex, Drugs, and Rock 'n Roll." The rock gods shared their stories about the struggle they faced day in and day out—staying with just one woman. Then they came to this piece with Alice Cooper. On the topic of marriage, he said something along the lines of "All these guys are wondering why their marriages aren't working out, and I tell 'em, dude you married a stripper, what did you expect?" As I sat there listening to this man covered in his wife's eyeliner I felt a thick mixture of anger, guilt, and embarrassment start to boil over in my blood. Not only had another stereotype been cast upon me because of my profession, but also my boyfriend of 2 months got to share in these words of wisdom, as he sat beside me on the sofa. I was so embarrassed I couldn't even look at him. Did he want to leave because of this guy's bullshit, or was he a secure enough man to see through that and love me for me, instead of my part-time gig. Maybe he sees me for the artist I am aspiring to be, not the means of getting there. Maybe he realizes that the best part of my work night, or any night for that matter, is coming home to him. Maybe deep inside he knows that. Maybe he loves me...maybe not.

Oh well. He ended up leaving me a week later. I guess he believes what "Alice" said. He said he couldn't be serious with someone who makes a living as a nude entertainer. And honestly, I understood. I can't blame some men for feeling that way. It's not easy, and whether I like it or not, there's a little truth behind what he had said. Some marriages with a stripper will not work out, period. Just like some marriages with a doctor, a lawyer, a policeman, a fireman, a banker, a pro athlete, or a burnt-out, washed-out, pickled old rocker in eyeliner won't work out.

In the end I realize that there is someone for everyone out there, whether you clean fish tanks for a living, teach children how to read, or take off your clothes. We all have this desire to love and to be loved. If there's such a thing as a soul mate, we want to find out who they are and what it's like to be with them. Look past your insecurities, love yourself, and others will too.

THE CUSTOMER

The men that come into strip clubs are generally nice guys; they often just want someone to talk to. Then there are the men that need to make themselves feel better or make the shitty day that they have had just a little brighter. These are the guys that come in and sit at the stage, having nothing but harsh words to say, oh how they love to laugh at us and call us names. They point out our flaws, and make sure that we know of them by the time the night's through. I remember one particular evening a " gentlemen" came into the club, and headed straight for my stage. His tie was all-amuck with a walk to match. There was a look in his eye that said a thousand words, all of which were filled with hate, anger, depression, and regret, and he was at my stage. " Take it off babe", he hollered as he waved crisp dollar bills in the air. By the time my song was finished I had made one hundred dollars off of him and was ready to make more. When I got back stage, the girls were already having a laugh over this disheveled gentlemen, and knowing how much money he was tossing around like bread crumbs in a duck pond, they were planning their attack. "Can you believe this asshole?" One by one, each girl began to share their experiences with this guy. And they were not all pleasant. Ok, none of them were pleasant! One girl began to describe her encounter. "I went up to this asshole and asked for a dance, you know what he told me? That I was too fat! Can you believe this loser? He's in here alone, on a Friday night, telling me that I am not good enough for him!!" Now of course this girl was not fat, she was actually quite beautiful, and very sweet. And the criticism did not stop there. He told another dancer to turn around only to shrug his shoulders and dismiss her as if she was repulsive. After watching this individual insult the majority of the women in the club, keep in mind, he was throwing his hard earned dollars around at the same time, it finally occurred to me why someone would behave this way. Why they would come into this club, pay twenty dollars, spend about another three hundred, and insult everyone in it. Let me tell you why, this is a guy who wakes up at some God awful hour to the sound of a piercing alarm, only to find himself being nagged by an unhappy house wife and screaming kids. When he finally escapes the madness of his HOME, and the happy married life, he finds himself sitting in his company car in bumper-to-bumper traffic, leaving time for him to imagine what his life could have been. After sitting in LA traffic for what seems like an eternity, he ends up at the job he detests, not the job he spent thousands on at college, while being bullied by an unforgiving boss. At the end of the day he sees that a twenty-dollar cover and room full of female strangers is a welcome way to let off some steam. For him, this is where he has power, and finally some control in his life (so he thinks). In actuality, it's the other way around. When we are on stage, we have control, that's why a lot of girls choose to dance. It's the one place, for some, where we feel confident and strong, sometimes dominant with a man.

For the most part, the life of a customer is a lonely one. Either their wife has left them, or it feels as if they have. I have heard so many sad stories of broken marriages, its no wonder why I question the idea of a piece of paper that tells you to love someone 'til death. Ninety-percent of married men that have come into the club were unhappy with their marriages. These guys would most likely cheat, or were trying to look for a DATE in the club. The other ten percent would usually sit there and say lovely things about their wife. They were there just to be a guy, watching beautiful women dance on stage. What makes their marriage work? They tell their wives where they have been. I believe that being in an honest, open relationship is far more important than a piece of paper, a white wedding dress, and a gold band. I think that when you have this in a relationship then you may be ready for marriage. But what do I know? I am just some stupid stripper right?

DEAR MOM

Before you sat down to read the pages of this book, I wanted to let you know how special you are to me, and how I think that you are the strongest women I have ever met in my life. I know that I may have done things in my life that you may not agree with. Heck, I have done some things I don't agree with. That's part of life. Making mistakes and learning from them, and believe me, I have learned. But there is so much I have learned from you. I have learned to be a tough independent woman from you. I learned how to open my heart to those in need thanks to you. You taught me how to appreciate the things that really matter, like family and friends, not riches. When you were forced to be a single mother, you did not give up. You showed me how a real woman reacts when a tough situation presents itself. Sometimes I sit around at night hoping and praying that one day, I will possess just half the strength you have inside.

DUCT UP

It was a Friday night at the club, around 8: 00 pm when the drama of the evening began to take place. As I left the stage making my way for the dressing room, I began to hear what sounded like an argument. I entered the room, which was named the "Princess Room". Every dressing room was named back in the seventies when the club was built and even after the years and through all the personal carvings you can still see the generous title. I cautiously pushed open the decorated door and was quickly assured that there was an argument taking place. " I know you took my dress and I want it back!" A half naked girl stood dead center in the dressing room, hands on hips, demanding the attention of every girl in there. Although we all had an idea who took the dress, you just never know in the dressing room. You can usually trust the girls, but sometimes someone sketchy oozes through the cracks. Like a cockroach in a family home they find their way in. When you're not looking they help themselves to your belongings, shoes, clothes, wallets, makeup, and anything else that tickles their fancy. Once they have robbed you blind, they split and head for the next strip club. Sometimes, they stick around to see what else they can get. You see, there are no cameras in the dressing rooms, well back then anyways. This would allow a new girl to come in, gain our trust, and share our clothes, conversations, booze, and some good laughs. Once she had that, she was in and the minute we turned our heads she would dip her deceiving hands into the bag of her choice. But that particular night was not going to go as planned for this cockroach. You see, I believe in karma, and when she chose that bag she chose her karma as well. The bag she plucked out of the bunch belonged to CHERYL. She was not just a sexy, beautiful exotic dancer; she was a badass southern girl who could throw down a bottle of whiskey while arm wrestling a sailor. Her hair was bleached blonde and teased and tossed. She looked like one of those big beautiful 80's video vixens you use to see on MTV, wearing tight spandex with sun tan lines that looked as if they have been painted on. Loud and always a blast, there was never a dull moment. If Cheryl was your friend, she was a loyal one, but if she were your enemy you'd better get out of town. At the time, one of her closest friends was Izzy, who was one of my friends. Now Izzy is one of the greatest friends I have, but crossing her is equally dangerous, so you can only imagine what a mistake it would be to cross both of these young ladies. Cheryl and Izzy both began to fancy this cockroach and they showed their affection by sharing their whiskey, and there was a lot to be shared. The cockroach drank and drank until it was time for it to go on stage. Rummaging through its bag to find an outfit, this cockroach slowly and carefully found its way to the stage. We all gathered around the stage to cheer the new girl on and lend some support like we do for all the girls. As the music began and the light show flashed the stage, from behind the curtain she came. Everyone cheered. Everyone but Cheryl. While the intoxicated cockroach stumbled on stage, completely unaware that she was wearing a dress stolen from Cheryl's bag earlier that evening, Cheryl gazed at her like a hunter gazes at its prey. For a second it went silent, all you could hear was blood boiling through her veins and the sounds of knuckles tightening. " That bitch is wearing my dress, the dress that was missing from my bag. She's dead!" She stood up and headed for the dressing room. To this day I still don't think I have ever seen a woman run that fast in high heels. One by one we all followed, this was going to be good. By the time we got to the dressing room, Cheryl had the cockroach against the wall, "So you like my dress do you? Well you're going to wear it all night BITCH! Izzy, hand me the duct tape!" Suddenly I felt like I was in a Martin Scorsese movie, and someone was about to be thrown in the trunk of a car and taken to the desert. "I could not help but laugh, and who could blame me?" I was about to witness a thieving stripper be duct taped to a chair. And that's exactly what happened. In the dress that it had stolen, the cockroach was taped to the chair drunk on her enemies' booze. After a few moments of amusement, humiliation, and warning from the so-called manager, Cheryl set the cockroach free. That night was a lesson to be learned for the cockroach and the other new girls of the Princess Room. We all may be princesses, but there is only one queen, and if you cross her you're going to get DUCT UP!

THE DRESSING ROOM

The dressing room in a strip club is where all the action happens. It is where you will find the girls being themselves. Backstage is the only place where we don't have to put on an act; it is where we discuss the mayhem of the night and mock the majority of the men that attend the club. Strippers and exotic entertainers are some of the best actresses in Hollywood. Night after night putting on an act for a crowd of men and sometimes women. As you exit the stage and make your way down the hallway to the dressing room, you begin to hear the cackles and laughter of the girls mimicking an unlucky fella. " Can you believe that loser, did his mom not teach him manners?" Sometimes I wonder what goes through a guys head when he disrespects a girl, anywhere, does he not know that there is a place where girls talk, a place where we discuss your stupidity amongst each other and then spread it like a plague. Well fellas, that's what the dressing room is to a stripper! So the next time you decide to say something offensive to a dancer just know that it's probably contributed to our discussion in the dressing room.

The dressing room is also a place where the girls go to relax. It's where we kick off the high heels and exchange them for some fuzzy slippers, light up a smoke, and sometimes quench our thirst with a gentleman of a different kind, good old Jack. For some this is where we look for quiet time, though it is sometimes hard to avoid the drama of the dressing room, you have to try. It often reminds me of high school with the little cliques. You have the popular girls; these girls are usually the moneymakers of the place. Blonde, big fake tits, the best clothes, expensive cars, and fancy jewelry to match. Like popular girls in high school, they often have some good-looking boyfriend as well. You have the alternative girls; the girls that play a lot of underground rock music, have generally more than one tattoo, and mostly dream of becoming an artist and dancing is supporting that dream. And last but not least the nerdy girls; yes, there are exotic girls that go to school. It's not just something that a girl tells you so you think that she isn't an uneducated stripper who was raised in a trailer park. When some girls are in the dressing room engaging in conversation, they are in the corner cramming for a test, or catching up on some reading. The truth is, there are lot of girls like this or girls that are a little bit of everything. I used to work with one girl that was all of the above; blonde, sexy, with some tattoos, great taste in music, and she was in school studying to be a biochemist. PERFECT! I used to look at her and tell myself, "This, to me, is the epitome of a perfect woman." She was smart, beautiful, fun, sexy, independent, and secure with her sexuality. What more could a guy want? Even she had a hard time finding a man. The dressing room is also where we would go for good "man" advice by the way. When you put girls in a room who are bored, with nothing to do, of course men will be the main topic. I couldn't tell you how many times I would see a girl crying in the dressing room over some guy who broke her heart. I remember when it happened to me. I was crushed. All I wanted to do was stay home, cry and eat junk food in bed. Instead I opted to go to work, and not because of the money or because I was afraid of getting fired! (By the way—Strippers don't get fired. We just leave.) I went in because I needed the company of the dressing room. I needed the comfort of the girls…my family. Shortly after arriving at work I began to heal, and soon after I was laughing and decided to forget about the heartache that I thought was going to be the end of me. I did it without the help of tears, junk food, or the warmth of my lonely bed. All I really needed was the warmth of the ladies in the dressing room.

CANDY MAN

For some men, a strip club is a place where they go to escape the loneliness that fills their days. And it's just not the girls that perform there that they find comfort in. They often know everybody that works there by name. That includes the security guards, the DJ's, all the managers, the lovely waitress, and sometimes even the cooks. There was this one customer that would come in three days a week. Monday, Wednesday, and Friday. He never missed a day, and if he did, we would worry, like a concerned father. That's what we were to him, a family. He was much older than most gentlemen in the club, probably in his late seventies. Every time I would get a glimpse of him it would put a small, but significant ache in my heart. Candy Man we called him, due to the fact that he always came in with candy and you would never catch him empty handed. It was the way he chose to consume the candy that was interesting. He would take a napkin and place it as if it were a tablecloth by opening it up and then spreading it across the bar. He would carefully place each candy in its designated spot, like a colorful candy platter at your grandmother's Easter dinner. I would watch him do this night after night, while letting my imagination wander. Why is he here? Does he have anyone in his life other than the men and women that work in this club, and is he happy? Sometimes I would just watch him from across the room, sitting with his candy platter as a look of gloom lay across his face. As the flashing, colorful lights dance around him and all these young, cheerful girls gather around him like a flock of seagulls on a sandy Florida beach, he seems to be in another place, forgetting about his surroundings. When he decides to finally seat himself at stage for a show, it is usually for one particular lady that he fancies. With long brown hair and a creamy soft complexion she is young and full of life…always smiling and cracking a joke or two. When he looks at her it's almost as if he is in a trance, with a gaze that looks like he wants to jump into her skin and live there forever. While the young girl swings around the pole, completely clueless as to what affect she has on this man, he tosses money out as if he is pleading to buy her soul. Then it occurs to me…yes he is there to see a beautiful woman dance naked, but he is also there to remind himself what it was like to be young and vibrant, with not a care in the world. Even a seventy year old man can see how for that moment on stage, we feel completely free and alive. When the show is over and the girl heads off stage, the old man finds himself right back at the bar, and once again enjoying his variety platter of candy, with a look of content upon his face.

These were the men that made my job easy. I enjoyed having conversations with them, where they would tell me stories of their past. For hours they would describe their lives in great detail, telling me about their wonderful wives who have long since passed away, and their children all grown up now with children of their own. And then there are men who have no one, they never married and never had children of their own. I will hear about their daily routine in great detail as well, from the time they wake-up until the time they go to bed. I find it funny how in their list of errands, like going to the bank the post office, and even the doctor's office, they throw in the strip club like it's a daily routine, and it is for them. When Christmas rolls around they are there to bring everyone a Christmas gift. When I say everyone…I mean everyone. The bouncers, the girls and even the valets get something. The gifts will vary, from perfume and makeup for the girls to candy and cologne for the men, and sometimes, just money. Oh there have been wacky gifts; there was this one gentleman who, at the time, in his eighties, was so old he needed a walker to get around. Like the Candy Man he too had a set schedule as to when he would come in, and boy he was there rain or shine despite the fact that he could barely move. He was a very sweet man, I remember him telling me how many girlfriends he had. "I had quite a few girlies in my day, one even looked like you, oh but she is dead now." He would tell me with his frail voice. He would also tell us that if it weren't for us he would be very lonely, and that's why at Christmas he was there with a gift for us. I remember one year Papillion received some lipstick. When he handed it to her he explained that because of his arthritis he could not wrap it, and that it was his favorite lipstick because his wife used to wear it all the time. Papillion did not want to be impolite by refusing the gift, seeing as it was his wife's old lipstick, so she gladly accepted the odd gift. Although it was generous to even give a gift, we all had quite a good laugh over the unique gift exchange.

THE AUDITION

The first time you dance on stage it feels like you are having an out of body experience. To this day I still can't remember it quite that well. Not to mention I had one or two shots of courage to pull me through. It was late, raining, and I was scared shitless. I had no "dancer clothes" to wear and the only pair of heels I owned was a pair left over from Halloween. When the cab pulled up to the club, there was a big flashy sign you could not miss, " LIVE NUDE NUDES", as opposed to dead nude nudes. As I stood there staring at the flashing sign, and as the rain poured down my face, smearing my poorly applied makeup, I wondered if this was the right decision. I thought of my mom telling me how these women will never get respect from others. I wondered how much this would disappoint her. I also thought of the bills I had to pay fast. "It will just be for a while and no one will ever find out", plus this rain was really starting to come down and I needed some shelter. As I sat in the back of the club waiting for my turn to audition, I couldn't keep my eyes off the gorgeous girls that filled the club. Everywhere you looked there seemed to be one beautiful girl after another pouring in from backstage. Sitting there, sipping my complimentary soda, I studied the girls from head to toe. I noticed their outfits and was shocked to see how high their shoes were, and I wondered how the hell they managed to dance in those shoes. Suddenly I felt like my Halloween shoes were not going to cut it. Before I could finish my soda, I was being whisked off to the dressing room. "This will be your locker, and you should lock it." With words of wisdom from the young manager I began my journey into the world of an exotic dancer. As I waited in the dressing room for my cue, one-by-one the girls introduced themselves to me. It was overwhelming; they were so beautiful and seemed to be having a great time, like a party. They all had their advice for me and other words of wisdom, everything from how to wear your clothes to how to dance on stage. They even offered me a cocktail to cool my nerves. That's where I first met Christy. She was just as new to dancing and, well…waiting tables there just didn't pay enough so she graduated to a dancer. Christy stood out from the start. With a short punky haircut and a bright smile she introduced herself to me right away, but not in a typical manner. "Do you have a boyfriend? Because if not you should meet my brother. He is awesome and I know his type and you are his type!" she asked with excitement in her voice. All I could think is, here I am, half naked, half drunk, and this girl is trying to set me up on a fucking blind date. Just as I thought of something to respond with I heard my name being called from the D.J. booth. "That's right fellas, put your hands together for MONICA!" As I stood there behind the velvety red curtain I was pondering the thought of this lifestyle, wondering if this is really for me. When you're young you sometimes don't think of the future consequences. You live in the moment, and at that moment I needed to pay rent. So before I headed to stage to embark on my radical journey, I looked back at Christy. "Yes, I am single, when I get off stage let's hang." And that was the start of a job, and a friendship that would last forever, and a relationship that would show me what true love really is.

THE LAST DANCE, THE DAY I QUIT

My last night working at a strip club was a sad one. Yes, I was happy; I mean this was something that I have wanted to do for along time. I just didn't have the guts up until now. But I had a lot of good memories in this place. Far away from the bar and way beyond the stage, behind a thick velvet curtain you make your way down a cold fluorescent lit hallway being guided by the sounds of laughter, tears, yelling and soon you find yourself in the dressing room. It's where I met most of my friends that have had the greatest impact in my life. This is where I learned how to talk to men, and how not to trust a lot of them, not all, but a lot of them. Although some were gone, Papillion went back home, Izzy was there, and she still to this day works her ass off, while helping everybody around her, as usual. And Christy, well she was definitely in a better place.

As I packed up my bag and emptied out my locker, I glanced around the dressing room one last time. It made me remember a time when I was working at this club in west LA. At that time, all the musketeers were together. Five days a week we worked, together. There were about fifteen girls working altogether, and we all, pretty much, for the most part, got along. But there was this one girl from France. It wasn't that she was a bad person or anything...it was just that she was LOCO. She had this crazy over the top laugh that when she got started she wouldn't stop. Her eyes would appear as if they were slowly trying to make their way out of her sockets. And her veins, the last time I saw veins like that I was watching an ironman competition on G4. They would pulsate on her forehead like they to were about to explode. But we still managed even with the incredible hulk of French strippers. So when one of us would move on, to do better things with themselves we were sad. I mean don't get me wrong; we were all very happy for them and very supportive. Even for the girls that, well, maybe it was not their time, and we knew that they would be back. You still support them because that has happened to all of us. You get all excited, get rid of your costumes, and follow it up with a night on the town to celebrate, only a week later you find that there are no jobs that will pay all of your bills, while still trying to make all your classes. So it's only a matter of time until you have to go back, for round two. But one night a girl left and she was never coming back, this we knew. She finished school, got a job (clothes required) and met her soul mate. She was getting married. We were all very happy for her as she left the dressing room for the last dance of her life, we all waved goodbye telling her to come back and visit, and one of us made a joke

"Come back for us, send help back." We all laughed, but inside we were right. We did feel like prisoners waiting for our turn to escape. Waiting for our prince charming to come and rescue us. But she never came back, and I can't blame her.

So now it's my turn to wave goodbye. As I glance around there are a lot of new girls who don't care that I am leaving. Like I said, a lot of my friends are not there, but I know that Christy would have been happy for me, and Papillion too. As I walk out of the club I look back to take one glance at the neon sign that boldly reads "GIRLS GIRLS GIRLS" and just then something happens. Something great happens! This heavy layer of stress, guilt and worry is lifted off my back. I am free, and most of all I can tell my mom that I am OK…and really mean it! The next day I got in my car with my best friend and, and my two dogs. As we headed for the mountains, off to our new home, I realized that it was time to start my life over again and recharge by bubble for the last time.

THE END